# COUNTRIES OF THE WORLD

# Canada

Gareth Stevens Publishing
**MILWAUKEE**

Bob Barlas has lived in Canada since 1962. He has taught in the Canadian and international school systems for over thirty years. Norman Tompsett is a native of Scarborough in Ontario, Canada. He has taught in the Canadian school system for twenty-seven years.

Written by
**BOB BARLAS** and **NORMAN TOMPSETT**

Edited by
**LEELA VENGADASALAM**

Designed by
**SHARIFAH FAUZIAH**

Picture research by
**SUSAN JANE MANUEL**

First published in North America in 1998 by
**Gareth Stevens Publishing**
1555 North RiverCenter Drive, Suite 201
Milwaukee, Wisconsin 53212 USA

For a free color catalog describing
Gareth Stevens' list of high-quality books
and multimedia programs, call
1-800-542-2595 (USA) or
1-800-461-9120 (CANADA)
Gareth Stevens Publishing's
Fax: (414) 225-0377.
See our catalog, on the World Wide Web:
http://gsinc.com

© **TIMES EDITIONS PTE LTD 1998**
Originated and designed by
Times Books International
an imprint of Times Editions Pte Ltd
Times Centre, 1 New Industrial Road
Singapore 536196
http://www.timesone.com.sg/te

**Library of Congress Cataloging-in-Publication Data**
Barlas, Robert.
Canada / by Bob Barlas and Norman Tompsett.
p. cm. — (Countries of the world)
Includes bibliographical references and index.
Summary: An overview of Canada, including an in-depth section on a variety of topics that make the country unique.
ISBN 0-8368-2123-8 (lib. bdg.)
1. Canada—Juvenile literature. [1. Canada.] I. Tompsett, Norman.
II. Title. III. Series: Countries of the world (Milwaukee, Wis.)
F1008.2.B33    1998
971--dc21                98-11227

Printed in Singapore

1 2 3 4 5 6 7 8 9 02 01 00 99 98

# Contents

# AN OVERVIEW OF CANADA

Canada is a country of great beauty. With mountains, prairies, and lakes, it is a haven for tourists, photographers, and nature lovers. Along with the United States, it shares the breathtaking Niagara Falls and the Great Lakes — the world's largest bodies of fresh water.

John Cabot, an explorer, sighted Newfoundland in the late fifteenth century. The arrival of more and more Europeans in the eighteenth century, however, threatened the existence of Canada's native people — the Indians and the Inuit. After decades of discrimination, they are now slowly getting involved in the government and holding their own in the arts. Canada today thrives on the coming together of its different peoples, not in a melting pot, but in a mosaic rich with many colors and textures.

*Below:* **Between 1991 and 1997, more than one million foreigners immigrated to Canada. There has been a large increase in Chinese immigration, and today Mandarin is the third-most common mother tongue in Canada, after English and French.**

*Opposite:* **Canada geese in winter.**

## THE FLAG OF CANADA

The flag was designed by Dr. George Stanley in 1965 in Ottawa. It is red and white, the official colors of Canada since 1921, the result of a royal proclamation by King George V of England. The maple leaf in the center is Canada's national symbol. It has twelve points. The two red stripes represent the Pacific Ocean and the Atlantic Ocean — two of the three oceans that border Canada. The flag reflects the common values of Canadians: freedom, peace, respect, justice, and tolerance.

# Geography

## The Land

Canada is the second largest country in the world after Russia. It has ten provinces and two territories (three territories in 1999). The area of Canada, about 3,800,000 square miles (9,900,000 square kilometers), stretches from the island of Newfoundland in the east to the border between the Canadian territory of Yukon and the U.S. state of Alaska in the west. Despite its size, Canada is home to only around 29,615,000 people.

Canada's climate varies considerably from region to region. The northern areas inside the Arctic Circle experience extremely long and cold winters. In the far reaches of the north, there are areas of permafrost where the ground remains frozen throughout the year and nothing can grow. While storms and high winds are characteristic of the Atlantic coast, the west coast has mild winters that are cloudy and wet.

There are seven separate geological regions in Canada, which account for the diversity of its scenic beauty. The Appalachian Region, which includes the east coast and eastern parts of Quebec, consists of hills and valleys created by volcanic activity millions

**NIAGARA FALLS**

**A famous spectacle, the Niagara Falls lie on the border between Ontario in Canada and New York State in the United States. Near the falls is Marineland, where dolphins and a killer whale perform. The world's largest steel roller coaster is also found here.**

*(A Closer Look, page 63)*

of years ago. The Interior Lowlands were formed by glaciers and cover most of southern Quebec and southern Ontario around the St. Lawrence River and Lake Ontario. This area is crossed by long ridges of high ground, such as the Niagara escarpment and the sand dunes near Lake Ontario.

The Canadian Shield, in the geographical center of Canada, is made up of ancient rock. More than six hundred million years old, it is considered one of the world's largest continental shields and contains almost a quarter of the world's fresh water supply. The Arctic Lowlands, the area around Hudson Bay in northern Ontario and northern Manitoba, is full of muskeg swamps, with stunted tamarack trees and black spruce.

The Great Plains, wide flat areas that cover the provinces of Manitoba, Saskatchewan, and Alberta, are called Canada's "bread basket," because much of the country's grain farming is done there. To the west is a mountainous region with alpine lakes. It includes the Rocky Mountains, the Cariboo Mountains, and the Coastal Mountains. Mount Logan, in the Yukon, is the highest mountain at 19,524 feet (5, 951 meters). The Arctic Archipelago includes the many small islands located off the northern coast of the country. Once a single land mass, the numerous islands have craggy coastlines dominated by cliffs and fjords.

*Above:* **The Rocky Mountains in summer.**

*Opposite, bottom:* **The Chute-Montmorency Falls in Quebec are higher than the Niagara Falls, at 274 feet (83 m). In winter, they freeze and become Canada's most popular wall of ice to climb.**

## THE ROCKIES

**The Rocky Mountains extend from Canada, south through the United States, down to Mexico. Mount Elbert in Colorado (U.S.) is the highest mountain in the Rockies, at 14,433 feet (4,399 m).**
*(A Closer Look, page 66)*

# Seasons

Canada's milder seasons are spring, summer, and autumn, while winter may be long and cold. Spring is one of the most beautiful times of the year — trees leaf out and wildflowers appear in forests and woods. At times, the weather is so changeable that sun, snow, and rain may appear on the same day!

Summer is usually very hot, with temperatures often above 86° Fahrenheit (30° Centigrade). Many Canadians go to the beaches to swim or vacation in their summer cottages. Rainfall is limited during the summer; at times, this leads to near-drought conditions in some areas. In autumn, trees lose their leaves in a brilliant display of color, and crops are harvested.

**ACID RAIN**

Acid rain is a serious problem in Canada and is harmful to plants, fish, lakes, and forests. It also affects adults and children, particularly those with respiratory problems.
*(A Closer Look, page 44)*

Canada's more northerly regions sometimes experience their first frost before the end of summer, and Canadians celebrate Thanksgiving the first weekend in October.

Winter is coldest in the northern and central plains. Snowfalls blanket large areas, which may remain white from late November to the middle of March. The far western parts of the country, with higher rainfall and temperatures, usually do not get as much snow. In the Arctic regions, in contrast, temperatures are below freezing almost all year round.

*Above:* **In parts of Ontario and Quebec, the reds and oranges of leaves turning color in autumn are so beautiful that many people go on special color tours to soak in the scenery.**

8

# Plants and Animals

Canada has many different plant and animal habitats, depending on the geological make-up and climate of the region. A particular animal or plant that is common in a province is often adopted as the provincial emblem.

Alpine plants, such as juniper and various kinds of lichen, grow in the northern parts of the country. They adapt to the short growing season typical of the cold, dry, and often windy regions by growing close to the ground. Their hairy or woolly leaves prevent water loss and provide insulation from the cold. The plants of the prairie region are adapted to the low rainfall and strong winds that affect central Canada. They have root systems that intertwine with those of other plants to form a thick root mat. This prevents the soil from being blown away.

The beaver, which lives in small communities and builds its home on lakes, is the symbol of Canada. The moose, a shy animal, is one of Canada's largest animals. Other animals, such as chipmunks, raccoons, and groundhogs are found in the eastern parts of Canada, living on the nuts and berries that abound there. Most famous among the birds is the Canada goose. Its distinctive honking can often be heard in spring and autumn when it migrates in large flocks. Other birds, such as blue jays and orioles, are found all over the country, while the majestic eagle is seen mainly in the mountainous areas of the west.

*Above:* **Wildflowers, such as trillium, are often the first sign of life in the spring, even before leaves are back on the trees.**

*Left:* **The wily Arctic fox seen here is found in northern parts of Canada along with caribou and North American wolves. Its startling white fur helps it blend in with the snow and ice in winter.**

9

# History

## Vikings and the First Inhabitants

The earliest people to reach North America were the Vikings from Iceland and Greenland. Historians believe that Leif Ericson, called "Eric the Red," landed at L'Anse aux Meadows on the northern tip of Newfoundland around A.D. 1000. However, Viking attempts at founding permanent colonies failed. Some remnants of Viking settlements can still be found in Newfoundland today.

Before the arrival of Europeans, an estimated two hundred and fifty thousand Indians and Inuit, descendents of prehistoric Asians, occupied what is now Canada. At the time of European discovery of North America, small groups of native people were living in western and central Canada.

## The First Explorers

The first explorers to come into contact with the native people of Canada were from England and France. They came to explore the unmapped areas of the New World. Explorer John Cabot ventured to the coast of eastern Canada as early as 1497. He was followed by the French explorers Jacques Cartier and Samuel de Champlain. Cartier landed in 1534 on Prince Edward Island and the Gaspé Peninsula, claiming the land for his native France.

## Fur Trade and French-English Rivalry

After the French claimed a large part of what is now Quebec as their territory, they sent several explorers to central Canada to look for fur, particularly beaver pelts. They were pleasantly surprised — Canada had a good supply of fur and pelts were nearly as valuable as gold. The explorers set up trading posts as they traveled inland, where tradesmen and priests settled. Gradually, new communities flourished.

The British, afraid the French would monopolize the fur trade, set up a special company, The Company Gentlemen Adventurers, to run the fur trade for them. They also sent their own explorers to Canada. Soon, they were in active competition with the French. In the north, the French faced rivalry from the Hudson's Bay Company, a British fur trading company, for control of the fur trade. In 1760, the French lost the battle of the

**SAMUEL DE CHAMPLAIN**

**Samuel de Champlain founded the city of Quebec in 1608 and established a profitable fur trade. However in 1611, the fur trade had heavy losses. He persuaded Louis XIII, the king of France, to intervene. The king made de Champlain the commanding officer of New France.**
*(A Closer Look, page 50)*

10

Plains of Abraham to the British, forcing them to give up their Canadian territories. In 1763, a treaty was signed in Paris whereby the French gave the rest of their Canadian territories to the British, except for the islands of St. Pierre and Miquelon.

# Beginning of Unification

Central Canada was divided into two colonies: Upper Canada and Lower Canada. The population in both grew as more and more people from Europe came to settle in the new land. As time passed, these people became unhappy with the laws and regulations imposed on them by the British government in London. As a result, two small rebellions took place in Upper Canada and Lower Canada in the 1830s. Most of the settlers, however, were keen to stay in the British Commonwealth and primarily wanted more independence over their own affairs.

In 1841, Upper Canada and Lower Canada were unified to form the Province of Canada. In 1848, the Province of Canada and Nova Scotia were given the right to self-government. Queen Victoria named Bytown (now Ottawa) the capital in 1857. A movement then began to unify all the provinces of British North America. In 1867, the Provinces of Nova Scotia, New Brunswick, Lower Canada (Quebec) and Upper Canada (Ontario) formed a confederation, from which the Dominion of Canada was born. Ottawa was the capital, and Sir John A. Macdonald was the first prime minister.

*Below:* **The lucrative fur trade of the seventeenth and eighteenth centuries.**

# Expansion

In 1868, Macdonald's government bought much of the land to the west of Ontario from a London-based fur trading company, the Hudson's Bay Company. After acquiring more land in the area from the British government, the province of Manitoba was created. In 1870, the Northwest Territories were acquired from Great Britain and became part of the Dominion of Canada. The colony of British Columbia became a province in 1871 when Macdonald promised to build a railway from coast to coast. Prince Edward Island joined in 1873.

## THE MOUNTIES

**The Mounties are policemen from the Royal Canadian Mounted Police (RCMP). Under their surveillance, the Canadian Pacific Railway was completed in 1885. At the turn of the twentieth century, they helped thousands of settlers to Canada cope with survival in the wilderness.**
*(A Closer Look, page 60)*

# Law and Order

Macdonald's government was concerned with maintaining law and order in the large, developing areas of central, northern, and western Canada. The Canadian government wanted to form its own police force there and so, in 1873, the North West Mounted Police (NWMP) was organized. In 1869 and 1885, rebellions against the Ottawa government were started by the Metis people in western Canada, descendants of the old French explorers and the native people. They were led by Louis Riel. It was not until the completion of the transcontinental railway that enough soldiers arrived in the area to finally defeat Riel and his soldiers.

# The Gold Rush and the Yukon

In 1896, George Washington Carmack and his Indian brothers-in-law, Skookum Jim and Tagish Charlie, discovered gold near the Yukon River in northwest Canada, sparking off a great gold rush. Some one hundred thousand people from around the world flocked to the Klondike gold fields to make their fortune.

By 1898, the Yukon was a territory of Canada. However, it remained isolated until World War II when the Alaska Highway was constructed. The U.S. army and Canadian engineers built the highway as an overland supply route to the U.S. forces. The Yukon today is slightly more populated than the Northwest Territories. About twenty thousand people live here; most of them are concentrated in the capital, Whitehorse.

# Unification Complete

People settled on the Great Plains of Canada after the completion of the Canadian Pacific Railway and a campaign by the Canadian government to bring in settlers with farming experience from Europe. In 1905, the new Provinces of Saskatchewan and Alberta were created. In 1949, Newfoundland, which was an independent colony of Britain, became Canada's tenth province.

*Above:* Gold was mined in the Klondike gold fields from 1897 to 1900. But by 1905, little gold could be found, and the population in the area dropped from forty thousand to five thousand people. Today, tourists to the Yukon can relive the days of the gold rush by panning for gold.

*Opposite, bottom:* Louis Riel was tried as a traitor and hanged, an act that outraged French-Canadians. At the Batoche National Historic Park in central Saskatchewan today, battle sites have been preserved, including a bullet-pocked rectory and the church of St. Antoine de Padoue. The grave of Riel stands here on a bluff.

# Jacques Cartier (1491–1557)

Jacques Cartier's explorations of the North American coast and the St. Lawrence River laid the foundation for subsequent French claims to Canada. In the hope of discovering gold, spices, and a route to Asia, he sailed into the Gulf of St. Lawrence in 1534 and landed on the Gaspé Peninsula. He claimed the land for France. Cartier made his second voyage the next year. He sailed up the St. Lawrence River to Quebec and Montreal. Because of war in Europe, Cartier made his third voyage to the new land only in 1541. He established a settlement that lasted until 1543.

**Jacques Cartier**

# Sir John Alexander Macdonald (1815–1891)

The first prime minister of Canada, Sir John Alexander Macdonald, was born in Scotland in 1815. He came to Canada with his parents at the age of five. The family settled in the town of Kingston. Macdonald was a colorful character and was a lawyer in Kingston before entering politics. By the 1860s, he had established himself as one of most influential members of the Conservative Party in Canada. He played a key role at the three conferences where the confederation of the provinces was discussed. Macdonald eventually became one of the signing "Fathers of Confederation." He served as prime minister from 1867–1873, and again from 1878–1891. He was most noted for completing the transcontinental railway.

**Sir John Alexander Macdonald**

# Alexander Graham Bell (1847–1922)

Alexander Graham Bell came to Canada from Scotland with his parents in 1870, at the age of twenty-two. Trained as a speech therapist like his father, Bell first settled in Brantford, Ontario. He moved to Boston in 1872, where he spent much of his time working on a device to help his speech-impaired clients communicate better with one another. In 1876, during the course of one such experiment with a transmitter, he spilled some acid on the front of his trousers and said the now famous words, "Come here Watson, I need you" to his assistant in the next room. Thomas Watson heard what Bell said through his end of the speech device, and the telephone was born!

**Alexander Graham Bell**

# Roberta Bondar (1945– )

Roberta Bondar is Canada's first female astronaut and as such, a role model for a whole generation of Canadian women. Bondar wanted to prove that women could do all the things that men had traditionally done, and just as well. She attended several Canadian universities, eventually becoming both a highly-qualified doctor and scientist. She was also a scuba diver, pilot, and balloonist. After being selected as one of the six astronauts in the Canadian space program in 1983, she was attached to the National Aeronautics and Space Administration (NASA) in the United States. She was a payload specialist on the Space Shuttle Discovery in 1994.

## EUREKA!

**A radio station for whales? Dr. John K.B. Ford, head of research at the Vancouver Aquarium, has started the first such station in the world. He believes whales have about a dozen calls and make noises to keep together in murky water. What about the popular game, Trivial Pursuit? Did you know it was invented by three Canadians?**

(*A Closer Look, page 52*)

*Left:* Space Shuttle Discovery's launch. After the voyage in space, Roberta Bondar described her extraordinary experiences in the book, *Touching the Earth.*

# Government and the Economy

## Government

Canada is the world's largest democratic country in terms of its land area. It has three levels of government: federal, provincial, and municipal. The federal government in Ottawa looks after the affairs of the country as a whole, including the environment, national defense, and foreign affairs, while the governments of the ten provinces look after the needs of the people, including education and health. Municipal governments in towns and cities are responsible for the day-to-day living of the people. The senior member of a municipal government is the mayor.

Canada is a constitutional monarchy. The Queen of England is the head of state and is represented by the governor general, who is a nominal head of government. The Canadian Parliament in Ottawa has two houses — the House of Commons and the

*Above* and *below:* **The changing of the guard, with new guards relieving guards on duty, takes place at the Parliament Buildings in Ottawa on fair summer days. The original Center Block was destroyed by a fire in the early 1900s. The new Center Block has a 300 foot (92 m) tower and a four-faced clock.**

*Above:* **The eastern part of the Northwest Territories will become the self-governing region of Nunavut, for the Inuit, in 1999.**

Senate. Members of the House of Commons are elected in general elections, which are held every four or five years or whenever the majority party is voted down. Several political parties run candidates in these elections. The party winning the most seats forms the government, and its leader becomes prime minister. The leader of the party with the second-most number of seats in the House becomes the leader of the opposition.

The prime minister chooses a cabinet of ministers and, together, they decide on the policies and bills to be presented in the parliament. Proposed laws are passed by a majority of the members of the House of Commons. The Canadian Senate, made up of senators appointed by the prime minister, then reviews them. Once approved, a bill goes to the governor general for his signature (primarily a formality), after which it becomes law.

Provincial governments work in the same way, except none of the provinces has a senate. Bills passed by provincial parliaments go directly to the lieutenant governor of the province (appointed by the governor general) for approval, although this is also a formality. Canada's far north consists of the Yukon and the Northwest Territories. They are administered by the federal government in Ottawa, although both have separate legislative assemblies.

## Trade

Canada and the United States manufacture many similar products, which leads to competition and sometimes conflicts between the two countries. A free trade agreement, or NAFTA (North American Free Trade Agreement), to work together to boost the whole North American economy rather than maintaining two completely separate economies has largely solved the problem.

Canada's Gross Domestic Product (GDP) ranks among the highest in the world. It is a member of the G7 — an elite group of seven countries, considered the world's most developed economies. Canada's biggest trading partner is the United States, but trade is increasing in volume with the European Union and countries of the Pacific Rim, such as Japan, Singapore, and Thailand.

## Agriculture and Fishing

Canada is one of the world's major producers of grain. Wheat, grown in the Prairie Provinces, is the chief export crop. On both coasts, fishing is an important export industry. In recent years, however, the output of processed fish is decreasing, the result of dwindling fish stocks.

*Above:* **Pulp and paper production is an important export industry. In recent years, Canadian engineers have helped developing countries build and operate their own environmentally-friendly pulp mills.**

## Natural Resources and Minerals

Canada is rich in natural resources. The forests in the country provide raw materials for the pulp and paper, lumber, and other industries, and provide jobs for 10 percent of the population. Alberta and the eastern coast of the country are known for their vast reserves of oil and natural gas. The value of mineral exports, such as nickel, potash, silver, and gold, is close to fifty billion dollars a year.

## Industry

In recent years, the manufacturing sector has grown to be the largest sector of the Canadian economy. Exports of manufactured goods, such as automobiles and forest products, provide jobs for over 16 percent of the working population. Canada also has a booming economy in high technology and finance. A number of Canadian firms are leaders in the development of new software products for businesses and the computer industry. In the past thirty years, the Canadian economy has almost completely changed from one that was based on natural resources and farming to one that is producing more finished products in factories located in big cities.

*Below:* **Golden bales of hay in Alberta's fields during the harvest. The province also has mineral resources, such as petroleum, natural gas, and coal.**

# People and Lifestyle

## A Mosaic of People

At the time of Confederation in 1867, the majority of Canadians were descendants of immigrants from England or France. The inflow of immigrants into the country from other parts of the world during the twentieth century has steadily changed that picture. Canada is now home to a great diversity of peoples, customs, languages, and religions.

Many Canadians in the Maritime Provinces of New Brunswick, Nova Scotia, and Prince Edward Island are descendants of the British who settled in the small coastal villages to harvest fish. New Brunswick is also home to many Canadians of French descent, while Nova Scotia is also home to the descendants of the original native people — the Micmac Indians.

In Ontario, Canada's most populated province, many people are descendants of the United Empire Loyalists, American supporters of the British during the American Revolution. They moved to Canada during and after the Revolutionary War. Since

**"BEES": WORKING TOGETHER**

"Bees" take place when friends and neighbors gather to help one another. They often have fun at the same time.
*(A Closer Look, page 46)*

*Below:* The Inuit, native people of Canada, will have a home of their own when Nunavut comes into existence on April 1, 1999. Nunavut in Inuit language means "Our Land." It includes Baffin Island, Ellesmere Island, and the surrounding region.

the beginning of the twentieth century, however, Ontario has seen the arrival of immigrants from all over the world. It is now the most ethnically diverse province. Northern Ontario is also home to the largest number of native Canadians.

The majority of people in Quebec are descendants of the French settlers who came to Canada in the early seventeenth and eighteenth centuries. British Columbia was originally home to the native people of the coast, such as the Haida, but now the population includes the British, Scots, and Chinese. Manitoba, Saskatchewan, and Alberta were settled mainly by immigrants from mainland Europe, especially the Germans and Ukrainians.

## Living in the South

Nine out of ten Canadians live in the southernmost part of Canada, not far from the border with the United States. This border is considered the world's longest undefended border and stretches over 5,600 miles (9,010 km). The most populated area of Canada is Southern Ontario.

*Above:* **The Chinese, who came by the thousands to help build the Canadian Pacific Railway, eventually settled in Vancouver. The city now has one of the largest Chinese communities in North America.**

### QUEBEC: THE CITY AND THE PROVINCE

**Quebec is the largest province in Canada. The capital is Quebec City. With more than 80 percent of the population speaking French, many residents want Quebec to be a separate country from the rest of Canada.**

*(A Closer Look, page 64)*

21

## Family Size

The average Canadian family is getting smaller. Canadians are getting married later in life, are having fewer children, and an increasing number of young people are leaving home to establish their careers elsewhere. Families with only one parent are also on the increase. In spite of this, most Canadians dream of owning their own home and the majority of people in the country do. Houses range from the mansions of the rich in the exclusive suburbs of major cities to the small and colorful homes of fishermen in Newfoundland. Some Canadians own two places — their main residence, often close to the place where they work, and a smaller cottage for vacations.

## A Typical Canadian Home

Most Canadian homes are built from a hollow wooden frame filled with insulating material to keep out the cold. Around this frame is an outer layer of brick or vinyl siding that gives the house its distinct look. The house is built big enough to house a single family, with two to four bedrooms, a kitchen, living room, and one or two bathrooms. Some houses in the countryside are so far apart that it may not be possible to see the neighbor's house!

*Above:* **A typical Canadian home in the city.**

**FAMILY COTTAGES**

**Nearly 80 percent of Canadians live in the cities. Many own a summer cottage, usually located near a lake, to escape the hustle and bustle of city life. The vastness of the country allows people to own more than one home.**
*(A Closer Look, page 54)*

Not all Canadians, however, own their houses — many in the big cities rent and live in apartments. These apartments are spacious and have all the conveniences of a detached house. In cities such as Toronto and Montreal, there are many large apartment complexes that share facilities, such as swimming pools and tennis courts.

## Public and Private Housing

Government-built public housing is available to those who cannot afford basic housing. Rents are fairly low. Government offices screen applicants to determine whether there is a true need. The houses and apartments tend to be a little smaller than the average Canadian home, but they are comfortable with basic facilities. The government has also built public housing for native Canadians in some places.

More and more older Canadians are moving into condominium apartment complexes with extra conveniences for residents. They feel safe with the round-the-clock security service. They also find it convenient to have the maintenance chores done by someone else.

*Below:* **"Habitat" is an award-winning condominium complex in Montreal, Quebec. It was the first major construction of prefabricated housing.**

# Education

In Canada, education is the responsibility of the provincial governments. Each province has its own Department of Education and its own system for training teachers. Public schools, which are supported by money from local taxes and government grants, educate more than 90 percent of the school-going population. Each province also has some privately-run schools. Education is free through high school.

At the age of three or four, young children may attend private day care or nursery schools. They go to elementary schools, starting in either junior or senior kindergarten. Students in rural areas travel to school in buses, while those living in the isolated areas of the far north may study either through correspondence courses or computer links.

Elementary school is kindergarten through eighth grade. From grades nine to twelve (or to grade eleven in Quebec and to grade thirteen in Ontario), students attend high school. In the ninth and tenth grades, a wide range of subjects are taught, such as English, mathematics, and science. Juniors and seniors are offered a wider

*Opposite:* **Students at a lecture in a university. Many young Canadians hold a part-time job for extra cash while studying.**

*Below:* **Teachers with their preschool children during an outing to the city hall in Toronto. By Canadian law, children must attend school from the age of six through sixteen.**

range of subjects, including computer science, technology, and trades courses, such as auto repair and woodworking, along with music, art, and home economics. There are special schools for students talented in science or the arts, as well as educational centers that attract students from all over Canada.

After high school graduation, students either get a job or continue their formal education at community colleges, technical colleges, or universities. Admission to these schools requires evidence of graduation from a high school and the achievement of a certain level of study. Courses at community colleges concentrate on practical skills training in areas such as agricultural technology, nursing, police work, and journalism. These courses usually take two or three years to complete, and the student receives a diploma. University courses take four years and a bachelor's degree is awarded. The University of Toronto and McGill University in Montreal are two major Canadian universities.

Education for adults is a growing business. Departments of Education, school boards, community colleges, and universities accept mature students who have been out of school for a number of years. Many part-time programs and correspondence courses are also available for adults.

### TERRY FOX CENTRE

**The Terry Fox Centre provides students with many opportunities to work together on projects. It is named after Canadian national hero, Terry Fox, who braved his handicap to raise money and awareness for cancer research.**

*(A Closer Look, page 68)*

# Religion

In early Canadian history, religion provided comfort to settlers in a strange foreign land. Churches were social centers, where people met and developed friendships. The English Canadians were predominantly Protestant, and the French Canadians Catholic. Although this religious divide caused trouble at times, Protestants and Catholics now live together peacefully.

# Native People's Beliefs

The native people of Canada practice a kind of spiritual animism that is deeply tied to the land and nature. In the past, they treated animals hunted for food with great respect and appeased a tree's spirit before cutting it down. Similarly, before eating, they appreciated the food for its life-sustaining sacrifice. Mythology played an important part in spiritual life, along with rituals.

When the French and English arrived in North America, they considered the natives to be savages who needed the "civilizing" influence of Christianity. As explorers ventured inland to develop the fur trade, missionaries followed to spread their faith. Today, the native people still struggle to maintain their beliefs.

*Below:* **Montreal in Quebec has many churches — 450 of them. The grandest is the Notre Dame Cathedral. Its stained-glass windows depict religious scenes and the early history of the parish.**

## Accepting All Beliefs

The cultural diversity of Canada has had its effect on religion in the country, which is also diverse. People who arrived after the French and the English settlers brought their own faiths with them. The Dutch established the Dutch Reformed Church, while the Scots, who emigrated to Nova Scotia in the nineteenth century, introduced Presbyterianism.

Canada has also been home to people who suffered religious persecution in their homelands. Oppressed minority groups, such as the Mennonites, Doukhobors, and Jews, who came to Canada from Russia, found solace and religious freedom in the vast Prairie Provinces, Ontario, and Quebec.

An influx of immigrants from Asia introduced Buddhism, Hinduism, Sikhism, and Islam. In fact, there are many mosques, temples, and synagogues across Canada.

Canadians are tolerant of the practices of different religions, and everyone is free to practice their own religion. They feel, however, that a person's beliefs should not be forced on others, and evangelism is frowned upon. The Charter of Rights and Freedoms protects people's rights to follow their beliefs.

*Above:* **Canada is home to many religions. This is a Sikh gurudwara, or place of worship, in Toronto. Sikhism, an Indian religion, was founded in Punjab, India, in the late fifteenth century.**

### MENNONITES

**Mennonites are the direct descendants of the Anabaptists, who lived in sixteenth century Europe. In 1663, Mennonites moved to North America to preserve their faith and seek opportunities for employment. They live all over the world, but are most highly concentrated in Canada and the United States.**

*(A Closer Look, page 58)*

# Language and Literature

## Official and Heritage Languages

In Canada, there are two official languages — French and English — that everybody learns. The English-speaking community is spread in a fairly even way across Canada, but the French-speaking communities are mainly concentrated in Quebec, New Brunswick, Ontario, and parts of Manitoba.

The Canadian Government sponsors school programs, such as French Immersion and English Immersion to encourage fluency in French and English respectively. In recent years, because of the large number of immigrants, a lot of different languages are spoken in Canada, including Mandarin, Vietnemese, and Hindi. Many schools now offer special heritage language classes for students in Polish, Mandarin, or Arabic.

*Above:* A sign in English and French illustrates Canada's bilingualism policy, which was adopted in 1969. English and French are both the official languages and were the languages of the original colonizers of the country.

## Distinctly Canadian

Canadian English is a little different from American English. This is true of the spoken and written language. Canadians pronounce words, such as "lever" (LEH-ver) and the letter Z (ZED) like the British. They have kept many of the British spellings as well, for example, "colour" and "centre." These language variations, however, do not pose a serious threat to communication.

The original colonists brought French to Canada in the seventeenth century. They came from different parts of France and spoke various dialects of the language. By the time the British took control of Canada in 1763, a French that was distinctly Canadian had developed. French Canadians today speak a language that is very different from the one spoken in Europe.

## French Literature

Much French Canadian literature grew from the folk tales and other stories of the early French settlers. The most well-known writer is probably Gabrielle Roy, the first Canadian writer to win the international writing prize for French writers, the *Prix Femina,* for her first book, *Bonheur D'Occasion.* The book was translated into English as the *Tin Flute.* The story was based on the experiences of French

## THE DIFFERENT TONGUES

The Canadian population can be divided into anglophones, francophones, and allophones. An anglophone is someone whose first language is English, while a francophone is someone whose first language is French. An allophone is someone whose first language is neither English nor French. New census data released by the Canadian Government in 1997 showed that for the first time, the number of allophones in Quebec exceeded the number of anglophones.

Canadian families living in one of the poorest parts of the city of Montreal. The book was an eye-opener for many Canadians, who were unaware that such poverty existed in Canada. Michel Tremblay and Marie Claire Blais are other popular French writers.

## English Literature

English Canadian literature dates back to the early history of Canada, with such personal accounts of life as *Roughing it in the Bush* by Susannah Moodie. The tradition of writing books about the communities in which one grew up was continued by Stephen Leacock, a much-adored comic writer, and by Lucy Maud Montgomery, who wrote the world-famous series, *Anne of Green Gables*, set in the Province of Prince Edward Island. One of Canada's best known contemporary writers is Michael Ondaatje. His book, *Running in the Family*, is an interesting account of the author's boyhood. Margaret Atwood is another Canadian whose books are admired by people all over the world.

## Native People's Stories

The native people of Canada, with their long tradition of storytelling and myths about how the world was created, have stories of their own to tell. The most popular of these is the tale of how the world was created by Sky Woman on the back of a giant turtle, with the help of all the animals in the Canadian wilderness.

*Below, left:* **Michael Ondaatje won a Booker Prize for his book, *The English Patient*, in 1992. It was later made into a movie in 1997, for which it won nine Oscars, including the one for Best Picture of 1997.**

*Below, right:* **Margaret Atwood was a Booker Prize nominee in 1996.**

# Arts

## Native Art

Native artists carved elaborately decorated totem poles, depicting the history of their tribes long before the arrival of Europeans to North America. The tradition of soapstone carving may be even older. It is still practiced by the Inuit living in the far reaches of northern Canada.

## Painting

Some European pioneer settlers, such as Paul Kane, who explored Canada's interior, made paintings of the native people, though in a very idealized way. The most famous painters in Canadian history are known as the Group of Seven. These seven artists, Lawren Harris, A.Y. Jackson, Arthur Lismer, Frederick Varley, Franklin Carmichael, Franz Johnston, and J.E.H. MacDonald, were inspired by the paintings of Tom Thompson, who painted the scenic landscapes of northern Ontario. Although he died before the group was formed, Thompson's name is almost always associated with these artists. In the 1930s, a group of French Canadian painters — Alfred Pellan, Paul-Emille Borduas, Jacques des Tonnancour, and Jean-Paul Riopelle — painted in a modern, experimental way.

*Above:* **An Inuit art sculpture by Mary Oshutsiaq. Sculptures such as these are now collector's items.**

*Left:* **An exhibition of Emily Carr's works at the National Gallery in Ottawa. Born in British Columbia, Carr painted the west coast Indians and landscape. She also wrote several books. She died in 1945.**

# Theater

Canada has a long theater tradition. Its proximity to the United States, however, has led to talented Canadian actors finding their fame and fortune south of the border. Among these Canadians are the famous silent screen actress Mary Pickford, the star of the *Bonanza* television series Lorne Greene, and Sir Christopher Plummer, one of the world's best-known classical actors. Many talented Canadian actors have also remained in Canada, so the theater scene is alive and well.

The most famous theater festival in Canada today is the Stratford Festival in Ontario, which honors the great English playwright, William Shakespeare. Another festival produces the works of George Bernard Shaw. Charlottetown festival performances of *Anne of Green Gables* are popular, as is the Banff Festival of the Arts, where actors from all over the world gather in the summer to display their talents in plays, ballets, operas, and concerts. Many big cities also have professional theater companies. Toronto, for instance, is a major center for staging musical productions before they go on to the bright lights of New York's Broadway or London's West End. Another city, Montreal, is home to the National Theater School, where aspiring young actors train.

*Above:* **The Place des Arts in Quebec is the most important center for the performing arts in Canada. The center cost millions of dollars to build and has five huge halls.**

## TOTEM POLES

A "ridicule pole"? This is the name of one of the seven types of totem poles carved by native people. In this pole, an important person who failed in some way has his or her likeness carved upside-down. Another, the portal pole, has a hole through which a person enters a house.

*(A Closer Look, page 71)*

## Film

Canada is known for the production of documentary and animated films; many are made with the support of the National Film Board. Atom Egoyan, a young Canadian director, is well-known for the quality of films he makes, while director David Cronenberg is famous worldwide for his horror movies.

## Music

Music of all types is popular among Canadians. This includes the music of different cultures, such as Jamaican reggae, African-American rap, Celtic folk music, and French ballads. Many Canadian cities often stage classical music concerts of a very high standard. Canadian musicians, such as jazz pianist Oscar Peterson and concert pianist Glen Gould have an international following,

*Opposite:* **The Royal Winnipeg Ballet is one of Canada's most famous ballet companies. It is known for its standard classical ballets and original works.**

*Left:* **Bryan Adams' songs are loved by people all over the world. One of his songs, "Everything I do, I do it for you" for the movie, *Robin Hood: Prince of Thieves*, was an international hit.**

as have the popular music stars Celine Dion, Bryan Adams, and Shania Twain. In 1996, Alanis Morisette won several Grammys, including album of the year for *Jagged Little Pill*.

## Dance

Canadians enjoy dancing. In many cites and towns across Canada, young people learn dances that range from the Scottish highland dance to the intricate steps of classical Indian dance, but ballet is probably the most loved dance form in Canada. Several well-known ballet companies, among them the National Ballet and Royal Winnipeg Ballet, have produced world class ballerinas, such as Karen Kain.

## Circus

Montreal's Cirque du Soleil is like no other circus in the world; performers come from many countries just for the privilege of taking part. A combination of theater performance and real circus, the circus uses no animals. Acts, woven together into a theme, are musically and visually exciting to watch. Performing under its own big top, the circus travels all across North America. It now has a permanent company in Las Vegas.

*Above:* **Anne Murray has four Grammys and two American Music Awards to her name. Her albums have sold over twenty-four million copies worldwide.**

# Leisure and Festivals

## The Great Outdoors Beckons

Camping is so popular that camping sites are found in almost all parts of the country. Many sites now have nearby shower and toilet facilities with special hook-ups for power and water. A number of Canadians prefer the convenience of tent trailers or mobile homes, the difference lying in the cost of the equipment and the luxury they offer.

With its many lakes and great expanses of wilderness, Canada is a hunters' and fishers' paradise. There are, however, strictly-enforced hunting seasons and catches are limited by law. Those who wish to hunt deer with a gun are required by law to take a special safety course before going on a hunting trip.

A fun way to spend time in the outdoors in the winter is to travel around the snowy countryside in a skidoo, or snowmobile, although this is inevitably accompanied by the din of motor noise and the smell of gasoline. For the ski purist, facilities for downhill skiing and cross-country skiing abound. In almost every part of the country — except on the vast flatness of the prairies — ski facilities are usually not far from the skiers' homes.

**BOMBARDIER**

**Ever wondered who built the skidoo? A Canadian invention, the skidoo was built by an auto mechanic, Armand Bombardier. His is a story of perseverance and the fulfillment of a dream.**
(*A Closer Look, page 48*)

*Below*: In the Rockies, downhill skiing challenges even the best skier. There are also fine downhill ski runs in the east, especially in the Laurentian Mountains north of Montreal and in the recreational area north of Toronto.

# Relaxing Indoors

Many Canadians spend much of their leisure time involved in projects to improve their homes. Many garages and basements contain workshops.

Other indoor leisure pursuits are equally popular with Canadians. Watching television, surfing the Internet and playing Nintendo are favorite pastimes. For some, collecting things is a passion — they haunt flea markets and auctions during the weekends. Others enjoy building model railroads or playing cards. Hobby shops, found in most cities, cater to all kinds of interests. Many clubs and associations in the country encourage people to start a new hobby or learn a new skill.

Canadians enjoy all kinds of crafts. For the newcomer interested in learning a particular skill, finding a teacher is usually not difficult because many of these crafts are taught in night classes. Local educational organizations sponsor these classes.

In the summer months in particular, local craftsmen display their items at shows and exhibitions, where articles of fine workmanship can be purchased inexpensively. Tourists and Canadians alike visit these places in the hope of a good bargain. Local art collectives run small, privately-operated craft shops that are open all year round.

*Above:* **Antique jars, candle sticks, lamps, and other old things in a Montreal flea market enthrall a bargain-hunter.**

# Hockey

There is no doubt that if there is a national sporting obsession in Canada, it is with the Canadian-invented game of hockey. In fact, many boys who enjoy playing hockey dream of becoming a member of one of the National Hockey League (NHL) teams.

NHL teams consist of both Canadian and American players, but many well-known players for all the major teams — among these, the Toronto Maple Leafs, the Los Angeles Kings, the Edmonton Oilers, the New York Rangers, the Montreal Expos, and the Vancouver Canucks — are Canadians. The top team in the annual NHL competition receives the Stanley Cup.

Watching a hockey game is an enjoyable pastime for many Canadians, whose Saturday nights are spent at the local hockey rink or in front of the television. The television program, "Hockey Night in Canada," is the longest-running television show in the country. Because the sport is so popular, it is difficult to find a time when the local ice surface is available for practice. Many Canadian parents therefore rise early in the morning to take their sons and daughters to hockey practice at a rink situated miles away from their homes.

*Below:* **Hockey is a rowdy game that sometimes leads to small fights between players from opposite teams. This, however, has not reduced the passion that players and spectators have for the game. Canadians simply love it!**

# Canadian Champions

Other international sports are played in Canada and have strong professional representation. Among these are track and field, tennis, basketball, squash, and lacrosse. Lacrosse, derived from a native game called *baggataway* (ba-gat-teh-WAY) is the oldest Canadian game. It is still played across the country. Young people learn to play sports at school, and the fundamentals are widely taught in physical education classes. Sports are also played in a league structure across the country, and leagues of some sports compete with U.S. sports leagues.

Canada is represented at the Olympic Games and other major championships. It has in recent years become particularly noted for its track and field athletes. In the 100-meter sprint and the 4 x 100-meter relay, there is rivalry between Americans and Canadians for the gold medals. The record for the 100-m, traditionally an event dominated by Americans, is now held by Donovan Bailey. He broke the record at the 1996 Atlanta Summer Olympics. He also anchored Canada's 4 x 100-m relay team to the gold medal. These victories helped erase the bitter memory of Canadian Ben Johnson, who was stripped of his 100-m title because of a drug scandal in 1988.

*Above, left:* **Donovan Bailey, a Jamaican-born Canadian, is the fastest man in the world. He ran the 1996 Olympic 100-m sprint in a world record time of 9.84 seconds.**

*Above, right:* **Canadian diver Anne Pelletier won a gold medal at the Pan American Games in 1995 as well as a bronze medal at the Atlanta Olympic Games in 1996.**

# Canada Day

Canadians love a party, and there are many opportunities to join in a celebration or festival. The most eagerly awaited party of all — Canada's birthday — takes place on July 1 every year. People across the country celebrate this special event in different ways.

The biggest party takes place in Ottawa, where the prime minister makes a speech and in a special ceremony awards Canadian citizenship to newcomers to the country. Toronto, Canada's largest city, sponsors a parade through the city center with a big, free picnic for its citizens. In 1992, there was more pomp and splendor on Canada Day than usual because it was the country's 125th birthday.

## The Calgary Stampede

Every year during July, the city of Calgary in western Canada hosts the Calgary Stampede, the biggest rodeo in the world! Cowboys from all over the world gather to display their skills in taming wild horses and fierce bulls, wrestling with young steers, throwing lassos, and racing horse-drawn chuckwagons. Chuckwagons are big wooden carts that cowboys used to live in when camping out on the open range. Cowboys in chuckwagons,

**WINTER CARNIVAL**

For many years, a snowman has been welcoming people to celebrate the wonders of winter from atop his Ice Castle. A crowd favorite, he is part of the festivities of the Quebec Winter Carnival. The Carnival attracts visitors from all over the world.
(*A Closer Look, page 72*)

*Below:* **Both children and adults enjoy painting their faces during Canada Day.**

pulled by a team of four horses, compete in the chuckwagon races — an adrenalin-pumping event, not meant for the fainthearted.

The Calgary Stampede lasts ten days. Other events, in addition to the rodeo, are held all over the city. These include pancake breakfasts, square dancing in the streets, colorful parades, and special western music performances in the parks. Visitors and Calgarians dress up as cowboys and enjoy the free chuckwagon breakfasts provided throughout the Stampede.

*Above:* **Chuckwagon racing was invented in the 1925 Calgary Stampede. The race runs in heats of four teams. At a signal, cowboys load tent poles and a box or barrel onto the chuckwagon and drive around a figure-eight pattern. They then race through a circuit.**

## Powwow

The festivals of the native people today are celebrated in much the same way as they were years before settlers from Europe came to North America. Different native groups celebrate in their own particular way, but they all have a festival called a *powwow* (PAU-wau). Before the *powwow* begins, a ceremony called the Grand Entry takes place. A parade, in which the leaders carry the Eagle Staff, moves toward a circle. Here, people dance to the beat of drums. The leaders are followed by the flag bearers, who carry the flags of all the native peoples taking part. Drummers beat their drums as the flags are raised. The native people sing songs, and the Grand Entry ends with a special prayer.

# Food

## A Bit of This and That

It is hard to define how Canadian food is different from American, British, or French food. Originally based on French recipes in Quebec or on British ones in other parts of Canada, Canadian dishes have since been influenced by Jewish, Italian, Russian, Greek, Indian, Chinese, and other cuisines. Immigrants to Canada brought with them dishes that have now become associated with the areas in which they live. There are some foods, however, that are native to Canada, such as the Saskatoon berry (a juneberry), fiddleheads, arctic char, and maple syrup.

### MAPLE SYRUP

If there is one food that Canadians identify as being totally Canadian, it is maple syrup. They pour it over pancakes for breakfast, churn out chewy bits of taffy with the sweet liquid, and even make mouth-watering ice cream.
(*A Closer Look, page 56*)

*Left:* Seafood lovers will not be disappointed when they visit Prince Edward Island. The province is known for its lobster dishes. McDonald's restaurants, for instance, have lobster burgers on the menu when lobsters are in season.

## Distinctive Dishes

In the Maritimes, seafood is commonly eaten, ranging from lobsters on Prince Edward Island to flipper pies in Newfoundland. Oysters and clams are popular, and the clam chowder is especially delicious. New Brunswick delicacies include fiddleheads, the young shoots of ostrich ferns. They are gathered from the woods in the spring, lightly boiled, and served buttered as a vegetable to accompany the main course.

The Province of Quebec has a number of special foods that have been served by French Canadian families for many generations. One of these is *tortiere* (tor-tee-EHR), a kind of meat pie traditionally made with pork and served on Christmas eve after the family returns home from church. Quebec also produces vast quantities of maple syrup.

Canadians in the Prairie provinces like Winnipeg goldeye, a small herring-like fish. The Saskatoon berry, which grows wild in the prairies, is used to make delicious pies. Because of the abundance of corn in the prairies, holding a corn roast with freshly picked sweetcorn is a popular activity. The west coast is noted for salmon, of which there are five kinds — chum, coho, pink, sockeye, and spring. There are also many types of game in the north of the province.

*Above:* **Canadians pour hot maple syrup over snow, and eat the resulting crunchy and delicious sweet ice.**

# A CLOSER LOOK AT CANADA

This section is an opportunity to learn more about Canadian life. The country has great natural wonders, such as Niagara Falls and the Rocky Mountains, as well as intricate native art and totem poles carved with birds, animals, and even beasts you have never seen before. Canada's history has been influenced by both the British and the French. Quebec, for instance, was one of the earliest French settlements. Three times the size of France, the Province of Quebec has the world's second-largest French-speaking city, Montreal. You can read more about the French

*Opposite:* **Winter has not stopped this man from doing what he loves: fishing. He has built himself a hut and is fishing through the ice. Canada is one of the best places in the world to fish, with many lakes and long coastlines.**

explorer, Samuel de Champlain, who founded Quebec City and about Quebec's unique culture.

People in Canada have fun in all sorts of ways. In summer, for instance, they head off to their cottages in the countryside. But winter does not stop the fun. You can meet the snowman in the winter carnival or zoom around on a snowmobile. Learn about listening to whales over the radio, watching the Mounties on horseback, and the array of things that make this country unique.

*Above:* **The Inuit are distinguishable by their Asian features. About 21,000 Inuit live in Canada.**

# Acid Rain

## Dead Lakes

Acid rain is a real environmental concern for Canadians. Rain, snow, mist, or fog are acidic when they contain a heavy concentration of sulfuric and nitric acids. These acids are produced when sulfur dioxide and nitrogen oxide gases mix with water. The gases are emitted from coal-burning power plants, metal refining industries, and the exhaust fumes of cars.

The worst acid rain areas are in Sudbury, Ontario, Province of Manitoba, and eastern Canada. Here, lakes are on granite rock and more sensitive to acid than some of the lakes in the west that are on limestone, which can neutralize the acid. In Sudbury, sulfur dioxide gases come mainly from the metal refining industries and electric utility plants. Pollution from the United States has added to the problem.

When acid rain falls on a lake regularly, it contaminates the water and affects the plants and wildlife in the area, producing abnormalities, such as deformed fish or stunted trees, and

*Below:* **Trees affected by acid rain can be badly damaged and are also more susceptible to other stresses, such as disease. In the Maritimes, a large part of the salmon habitat has been lost because of acid rain pollution.**

eventually killing them. Lakes that have been exposed to acid rain for a long period of time can actually become "dead," containing no fish and very little plant life. People who drink the water also put themselves in danger. What is more, acid precipitation also corrodes buildings and metal structures.

## The Solution

Acidic gases often mix into the normal cloud formations in the air, making the clouds acidic. The clouds may move some distance before the poisonous mixture falls to the ground as acid rain. So, it is very hard to pinpoint the actual source of the pollution. This sometimes causes disagreements between the United States and Canada as to who should take the blame for acid rain, but both sides agree that it is a problem they share, and that a solution has to be found.

Factories now try to reduce sulfur dioxide emissions by installing special scrubbers on their chimneys so that harmful gases do not escape. They also use different fuels. All North American cars are now required to have filters. In 1991, Canada and the United States finally established an Air Quality Accord to control emissions. In some parts of Canada, lakes are actually coming back to life.

*Above:* **More than fourteen thousand lakes in Canada have become acidic since the problem of acid rain became serious in the 1970s; some are completely dead. This lake in Saskatchewan is one of the lakes in the country not affected by acid rain. It provides plenty of opportunities for fishing, water sports, and wildlife viewing.**

# "Bees": Working Together

## Helping One Another

The idea for "bees" began during the Pioneer Days in Upper Canada when people got together to make some contribution to the progress of the community or to perform a service for one of their members. Modeled on the swarming behavior of the honey bee, this gathering of neighbors and friends is still practiced in some rural communities, especially if there is a large project requiring extra manpower or if help is needed for a disaster victim. Originally, there were all kinds of occasions that called for the holding of "bees" — erecting farm buildings, harvesting (the most common), logging, and the communal butchering of farm livestock.

Farm wives hold quilting or knitting "bees" among themselves, often at the same time as the men are outside working on a project. Children and other young people participate, too, helping parents with the preparation of the food and serving. These chores become fun and are usually done without complaints during "bees."

*Below:* **An otherwise boring job becomes interesting when everyone pitches in to help.**

## A Time to Socialize

A big, scrumptious meal is served by the women when the work is completed. In the evening, with the youngest children tucked in bed, young men indulge in trials of strength, watched attentively by young ladies. The older men discuss the prices of crops, local politics, and the prospects for the coming year, while their wives update one another on the happenings in their families, such talk sometimes extending to the latest news in the neighborhood. The young and the young-at-heart then prepare themselves for a night of dancing and country games.

*Above:* **A quilting session in progress. Many women get together during their free time to make the quilts. A big quilt sometimes requires the skills of more than one person.**

## Changing Times

Rural communities have undergone many changes since the last century, and "bees" are not held as often these days. However, many activities associated with the "bees" are still held in the clubs of some of these communities. For instance, there are quilting clubs, in which many women are active members. For the teenagers, there is the 4H Club. It sponsors courses on the raising of livestock, cooking, and sewing. The results of these activities are often exhibited during autumn fairs.

# Bombardier

## A Stroke of Genius

A small garage in Valcourt, Quebec, was the launching pad for Armand Bombardier's career. He is credited with turning his hometown from an agricultural town into an international industrial center. An auto mechanic, Bombardier was intrigued by the idea of a machine that could easily travel on Canada's snowy winter landscape. Roads then were not usually plowed in the winter, making traveling by cars almost impossible. So in the 1920s, he built the first snowmobile, the SKI-DOG, that could ski over snow. This soon evolved into the skidoo or snowmobile — a car-like machine with tracks like a tank. In the 1930s, after many refinements, he started producing them for others.

## The Ultimate Winter Vehicle

The snowmobile provides lots of fun for the whole family. People can use it to explore the vast snowy expanses and frozen lakes of Quebec and other parts of Canada during winter. The snowmobile is also used by racers in competitions. The

*Below:* **Although the snowmobile is a fun means of travel, some people complain of headaches and nausea, which they believe are caused by the fumes and noise from the vehicles. As a result of these complaints, alternate fuels for the snowmobiles are now being considered.**

Snowmobilers' Clubs organize many races and events all year long, such as the North American Snowmobile Festival. In the far north, it is the main form of transportation, replacing the dog team and the sled. The snowmobile is even used for Arctic and Antarctic expeditions!

Quebec, the snowmobile capital of the world, has over 18,600 miles (30,000 km) of trails, including the 5,600 miles (9,000 km) of the Trans-Quebec network that winds through almost every corner of the province. Along the clearly marked trails, snowmobilers can find everything they need, from fuel and repairs to food and lodging.

*Above:* **Bombardier's aircraft play an important role in fighting forest fires.**

## Conquering the Land and the Skies

Bombardier's company is now one of the biggest in Canada and produces many other products, besides the snowmobile, that help transport Canadians and people all over the world. In 1974, Montreal gave the company a multi-million dollar deal to build subway cars. In 1988, the seadoo personal watercraft for traveling on lakes and rivers was launched. In 1996, the company unveiled the Neighborhood Electric Vehicle for short trips in suburban areas. Recently, the company sold twenty-five of its new seventy-seat regional jets to American Airlines.

# Samuel de Champlain

## Braving the Unknown and Making Waves

In 1605, French explorer Samuel de Champlain founded Port Royal (now Annapolis Royal), the first permanent European settlement in North America. This settlement is located in what is now the Province of Nova Scotia. Champlain later went on to become one of the most prominent figures in Canadian history and is sometimes fondly referred to as "The Father of Canada." The first governor of New France (the French colonial empire in North America), Champlain encouraged French settlers to come to Canada and settle. He died of a stroke in Quebec City on Christmas Day, 1635.

Born in Brouage, France, Champlain was a sailor early in his life, traveling first to the West Indies and Mexico, and then spending the rest of his life making expeditions into the interior of central Canada. He first explored the St. Lawrence River and traveled as far as Montreal Island. In 1604, he founded the first white settlement at the St. Croix River in New Brunswick, and in July 1608, he founded the city of Quebec. *Kebec* (ki-BEK) in

*Above:* **Canada is still involved in the fur trade. This is a fur trading post at Hudson Bay in British Columbia.**

## TRADING FURS

Many young men disappeared for years to trade with the Indians in Canada's interior. The late seventeenth century saw fur traders, the *coureurs des bois* (koo-rer-de bwah, literally "runners of the wood") setting out across the continent in search of furs.

*Left:* **A statue of Samuel de Champlain in Quebec City. In 1609, Champlain discovered a lake in Quebec, which was later named after him.**

Algonquian Indian means "place where the river flows." Establishing his base at Quebec City, Champlain began making maps of New France and explored farther inland.

## Friends for Fur

On reaching the Great Lakes, Champlain started a fur-trading network with the Algonquian and Huron Indians to bring the furs through Quebec and ship them to markets in France. He supported the two Indian tribes in their wars against traditional enemies, such as the Iroquois. As a result, the Iroquois later sided with the British in their successful struggle with the French for control of New France. The fur trade, however, suffered heavy losses in 1611, so Champlain persuaded Louis XIII to appoint a viceroy. The viceroy later made him the commanding officer of New France. In 1613, Champlain embarked for the Ottawa River to restore the fur trade and in the following year, he formed a company of French traders to finance trade, religious missions, and his own explorations.

*Above:* **The European settlement of St. Marie Among the Hurons, in present-day Ontario, was abandoned in 1649 because of the Iroquois Wars. This was a series of conflicts between the Iroquois and the French, who had Huron and Algonquian Indian allies.**

# Eureka!

## From Zipper to Trivial Pursuit

In the 1940s, Dr. Gideon Sundbeck of the Lightning Fastener Company in St. Catherine's, Ontario, came up with a quick way to keep much of our clothing together. He adapted the old slide fastener into the modern zipper. Although Dr. Sundbeck was not the first person to think of the idea, he was the first person to make it work and sell the idea to others. Other Canadian inventions include the paint roller, invented by Norman Breakey of Toronto in 1940, and the snowmobile, invented by Quebec auto mechanic, Armand Bombardier.

Canadian inventions in the medical field include the electron microscope, which was developed at the University of Toronto, and the drug insulin, commonly used to control diabetes. Insulin researchers received the Nobel Prize in chemistry for their work. In the field of technology, Canada's National Research Council developed Canadarm, one of the world's most advanced robots. Trivial Pursuit — a game loved by people all over the world — was invented by three young Canadian men in just forty-five minutes! They subsequently became millionaires.

*Below:* **The RADARSTAT, developed in Canada, is the world's first commercial satellite that "sees" through clouds and darkness.**

*Above:* **The orca, or killer whale, is a common sight in the waters of British Columbia.**

# New Way to Surf

In 1997, the Canadian phone company, Nortel, and a British electricity supplier announced that they had come up with a new method of accessing the Internet — via ordinary electricity supply cables. This breakthrough means low cost and high speed access to the Internet compared to using telephone lines or cable television circuits. Internet users can now pay their access bills together with other electricity charges.

# Radio Station for Whales

In 1997, Marine scientist K.B. Ford started ORCA-FM, the world's first all-whale radio station. Using a low-power FM license, he intends to broadcast continuously from under Robson Bight, a stretch of sea between British Columbia and Vancouver Island — one of the busiest killer whale intersections in the world.

The radio transmissions will help scientists understand how killer whales live. Presently, the transmission area of the all-whale radio is limited to a 10 mile (16 km) radius of Robson Bight. This will allow the people who come in whale-watching boats each year to listen and understand how their presence affects the whales. There were 107 whale-watching boats alone at Robson Bight during one day in the summer of 1996.

# Family Cottages

## Call of the Wild

Many Canadians live in an urban environment. The percentage of urban population, however, differs from one province to another. Most of the country's urban population is in Ontario, British Columbia, and Alberta.

Canadian cities have a central downtown area for business activities. Surrounding the business district are residential areas, where houses, shopping centers, and other amenities are located. City living is fast-paced and exciting. Entertainment is available day and night, but many Canadians find that life in big cities sometimes gets too stressful. For those who live in apartments, summer brings with it a longing for a way of life that just is not found in the towns and cities. For this reason, many Canadians own a "summer cottage," a home away from home that is a prized possession. Here, they find peace and tranquility in the company of loved ones.

*Below:* **One of the many summer cottages in Canada. The lake beside the cottage is a beautiful spot to canoe, one of Canadians' favorite recreations.**

Some cottages remain in the same family for several generations, while others change hands regularly, but they all share the same basic purpose — to give their occupants an opportunity to get away from the hurried pace of their ordinary lives and spend time doing things they like. These include fishing, canoeing, water-skiing, sailing, and socializing with friends and neighbors, or simply hanging out enjoying the summer sun.

*Above:* **Summer cottages, ranging from simple cabins to mansions, dot the scenic Thousand Island region of the St. Lawrence River in Ontario.**

## A Popular Getaway

Cottages take many forms — from a simple one-story structure, often without a telephone, but usually with some kind of electrical and water supply, to a building that can be as complex as a permanent home. Summer cottages are often located next to some body of water, for instance, near the many lakes found in the country, particularly in the Canadian Shield.

Cottages are usually used only as weekend residences — the busy traffic in major cities on Friday and Sunday nights show this clearly. In the summer, some Canadians may choose to live in the cottage during the week, especially during school vacations. Most Canadians plan their summers around weekends at the cottage.

# Maple Syrup

## How Maple Syrup Is Made

Canadians, especially those living in the eastern part of the country, think of maple syrup as a Canadian speciality. Used by Canadians from coast to coast all year round, maple syrup is a favorite on breakfast pancakes.

As winter nears its end, "sugaring off" begins. During this process, maple syrup producers "tap" the maple trees in their sugar bush, a grove of sugar maple trees, by drilling a hole in the trunk of the tree and inserting a special tap called a spigot. A bucket is then hung underneath the spigot to collect the sticky liquid — maple sap — that flows up the tree from the roots. Sometimes, the spigots are connected together by a special hose, which leads directly into the nearby sugar shack. The sugar shack is often a small wooden building with a tin roof and a large metal tank in the center heated by a wood fire underneath. The maple sap is then boiled in the tank for several hours until most of the water in it evaporates. The maple syrup is ready!

*Below:* **A boy checks whether the buckets on a sugar maple tree are full. The sap from the tree is sweet and sticky, but thin. It takes many gallons (liters) of sap just to make a gallon (3.8 liters) of syrup.**

# Maple Syrup Festivals

The annual sugaring off is often an occasion for celebration in small towns and villages where the sugar bushes are located. In early March, Ontario and Quebec hold maple syrup festivals. During these festivals, maple syrup is produced and enjoyed in many different ways. For instance, children make maple taffy simply by pouring a little hot maple syrup on the snow and eating the resulting sticky mass when it cools. Other exciting events in the festivals are horse-drawn sleigh rides, log sawing contests, and snowshoe races.

*Left:* **Children love maple syrup, since they can make their very own sweet treats with it! This young girl has poured syrup on ice to make some sticky taffy.**

# Mennonites

## A Way of Life . . .

Originally from mainland Europe, particularly Germany, Mennonites settled in communities throughout Canada, especially in Ontario and the prairie province of Manitoba. Until the late nineteenth century, they lived mostly in rural communities and were successful farmers. There are around one hundred and ninety thousand Mennonites now in Canada, and all of them are strict Christians. Not baptized until they are adults, Mennonites believe in the voluntary following of the faith and worship God according to their own tradition. Once baptized, they commit themselves to a code of strict behavior. They have no priests; they believe that every adult Mennonite carries the spirit of God within himself or herself. Important decisions are made by the community as a whole.

Some Mennonites in Canada belong to the "Old Order," which believes in a set way of doing things. They do not use cars or modern appliances, such as telephones or televisions; they prefer to lead their lives in the traditional way, such as getting around by horse and buggy, following traditional pastimes, such as quilt making, and

*Below:* **The Mennonites take their ideas and beliefs about the way that they should live from the teachings of a fifteenth century Dutch Protestant leader, Menno Simons.**

attending prayer meetings. "Old Order" Mennonite children usually do not attend public schools or universities. They are either taught at home or attend special schools set up by the Mennonite communities. They do not marry outside their communities, either. The Hutterite Brethren, who live in the Great Plains, still live communally and practice community of goods.

*Above:* **In Steinbach, Manitoba, Mennonites celebrate their heritage during Pioneer Days. They dress up as traditional farmers and display their threshing and baking skills.**

## That Is Slowly Changing

Not all Mennonites follow such a strict path of living. Some Mennonite communities allow their members to choose their own lifestyle and mode of transportation. Members of these communities send their children to school. They realize the importance of higher education and give a lot of support, especially to their own colleges and seminaries. They also interact with the surrounding community as a whole by voting in elections, serving in elected government positions, and being active in international charity work.

The Mennonite Central Committee, founded initially in 1920 to relieve famine in Russia, is now involved in a lot of charity work both in Canada and abroad, helping people of less fortunate circumstances. Many of these Mennonites have also married outside their faith.

# The Mounties

## Protectors in Red

The Royal Canadian Mounted Police (RCMP) was founded in 1873, initially called the North-West Mounted Police, and given the task of maintaining law and order in the newly settled western and northern parts of the country. The lawlessness that accompanied the opening of the American West was very much on the minds of lawmakers when creating the police force. They were determined to bring lawbreakers to justice as swiftly as possible. By and large this worked, mainly because there were very few occasions when the Mounties did not succeed in bringing in those guilty.

When gold was discovered in the Klondike, the North-West Mounted Police were sent at once into the Yukon. They maintained order, so it was the most organized and controlled gold rush in history. The legend of the Mountie in the scarlet tunic and the distinctive hat, who always got his man, thus began.

Today, there are detachments of Mounties all over Canada. In all but two Canadian provinces, they are completely responsible

*Below:* **The Mountie is known all over the world as a symbol of Canada.**

*Above:* **The RCMP officers at the Fort Macleod Museum in Alberta.**

for the enforcement of law, and even in Ontario and Quebec, which have provincial police forces dealing with offenses, they remain responsible for administering all the laws passed by the Parliament in Ottawa. The RCMP sponsors the Canadian Police College, which is attended by selected members and non-members of the force.

## Entertainers with Style

The Mounties are present at all ceremonial events, from the large parties that the governor general holds at his residence in Ottawa to the citizenship ceremonies held across the country, where immigrants to Canada formally become citizens.

The Mounties do not use horses in their regular activities anymore because patrol work is done in cars like in all other police forces. However, a special section of the mounted police is kept for ceremonial purposes. The RCMP's musical ride, in which the Mounties and their horses perform special maneuvers to music, is very popular. Children especially enjoy watching their well-timed and exciting acts. These are performed all over Canada on special occasions during the year.

# Niagara Falls

## Thundering Rapids

One of the greatest natural wonders of the world, the Niagara Falls are actually two major waterfalls that thunder over the edge of a mid-river cliff and drop vertically, sending tons of water every minute into the Niagara River Gorge. The American Falls is a little higher at 190 feet (58 m) than Canada's Horseshoe Falls at 185 feet (56 m), but it is much smaller in width. The Horseshoe Falls also has a much larger volume of water flowing over it. Since 1896, it has been used to generate electricity for the people of Ontario and for those in the nearby city of Buffalo in the United States.

## Daredevil Antics

Many people have tried to ride over the Horseshoe Falls, and although it has proved fatal for some, there have been many spectacular successes. Annie Edison Taylor was the first, going over in a barrel in 1901. Since then, others have gone over in various containers, such as rubber balls and metal containers. Many have also tried to cross the falls on a tightrope, including the famous daredevil, Albert Blondin. There is now a special museum at Niagara Falls that contains much of the equipment used by daredevils.

*Opposite:* Niagara Falls attracts tourists from all over the world every year, but it is particularly popular with honeymooners. The brother of the famous Napoleon Bonaparte supposedly traveled all the way from New Orleans in the southern United States to Niagara Falls to honeymoon with his American bride.

*Left:* A ride on one of the Maid of the Mist boats takes visitors up the gorge to the bottom of the falls. Raincoats are provided for these wet, deafening, but exciting rides.

# Quebec: the City and the Province

## Cradle of French Civilization

Quebec City is the provincial capital of Quebec and is the oldest city in Canada. It lies 155 miles (250 km) northeast of Montreal at the mouth of the St. Charles River, where it flows into the mighty St. Lawrence River. It has a population of just under two hundred thousand people, most of whom speak French.

The oldest part of the city was founded on a promontory above the St. Lawrence in 1608 by Samuel de Champlain, who also built a fort on the edge of the river. During the time the French were active explorers in North America, Quebec City was the center of their activities. After it was captured by the British in 1759, it became the capital of the new British colony of Quebec, and subsequently the capital city of the province of Lower Canada. At the time of Confederation, it became the capital of the Province of Quebec.

*Below:* **Quebec City, the capital of Quebec, is North America's most European city. It has winding streets, distinct French cafes, stone buildings, and public squares.**

Today, Quebec City still has many of its older buildings, including the Citadel and the huge hotel, the Chateau Frontenac, built in the style of an old French castle. The old part of town maintains the character of earlier centuries, but, Quebec is also a modern city, with high-rise buildings and office towers.

*Above:* **In Quebec, the movement for separation from Canada is still alive. Graffiti and street posters demand "liberty."**

## The Separatist Movement

Over the centuries, the Province of Quebec has developed a different culture, cuisine, language, and literature. Many French Canadians consider the province a "distinct society" within Canada and want Quebec City to be the capital of an independent country. Two referendums have been held in the province on this subject, although the option of leaving Canada and becoming a separate country has never attracted enough votes.

The political leadership in Quebec, the Parti Québécois, wants to hold yet another referendum before the turn of the century to settle once and for all whether Quebec should be an independent country, maintaining some economic links with the rest of Canada if possible, but being separate and distinct in all other areas. The party, formed in 1968, wants to retain links, such as a common currency. In 1995, voters in Quebec narrowly rejected separation by a margin of just over 1 percent.

# The Rockies

## Majestic Mountain Range

The area commonly known as the Rocky Mountains is actually several separate mountain ranges that extend from the Yukon south through the western United States to Mexico — a total of 3,000 miles (4,800 km) in all. Early explorers called the Rocky Mountains "a sea of mountains," with its many jagged peaks covered with blue ice and white snow.

Banff, Canada's oldest park, was founded in 1855 when sulfur hot springs were discovered in the Rockies. The original Mountain Park was expanded to become the Banff National Park, which includes Lake Louise, a beautiful turquoise lake set amid snowcapped peaks. Visitors can ride gondolas to three mountain lakes for a panoramic view of the surrounding peaks and river valleys. The Sulfur Mountain Gondola, built solely for sightseeing, ends at a 360-degree observation deck and a three-tiered restaurant, the highest in the Rockies.

*Below:* **The Rocky Mountains attract sightseers, tourists, and trekkers all year round. There are also opportunities for downhill skiing and cross-country skiing.**

## Ice Tours

Another scenic wonder, the Columbia Icefields, lies on the 143-mile (230-km) north-south parkway that connects Lake Louise and the town of Jasper. Once part of a huge sheet of ice that covered Canada for more than a million years, the Columbia Icefields is a huge glacier with an area of 125 square miles (325 square km). In some places, the ice is over 984 feet (300 m) deep. For those interested in a closer look at the icefields, tours are offered by snowcoach — a special vehicle that takes people right onto the ice surface.

*Above:* **The thrill of white water rafting attracts many people to the Rockies.**

## Flora and Fauna and More

White spruce, aspen, fir, and alpine meadow grasses cover the mountains, while grizzly bears, brown bears, moose, bighorn sheep, and mountain goats roam through many of the national parks, such as the Yoho, Jasper, and Banff national parks.

Beside soaking in the scenery, horseback riding, hiking, and white water river rafting are popular sports with Canadians and tourists alike. Hot springs, natural bridges, grottos, and even ghost towns are the other attractions in the Rocky Mountains.

# Terry Fox Centre

## Triumph of Mind over Body

Between April and September 1980, Canadians followed the progress of one young man as he moved slowly across Canada. Terry Fox was then twenty-two years old. Three years earlier, when he was a student and well-known athlete at Simon Fraser University in British Columbia, his right leg was amputated

*Left:* **Terry Fox raised more than a million dollars for cancer research by running across Canada. However, he died in 1980 before he could complete the run. The Terry Fox Run now takes place in as many as fifty countries each year.**

because of bone cancer. He was fitted with an artificial leg. From then on, Terry wanted to do something to help other victims of cancer in Canada. In 1979, he wrote to the Canadian Cancer Society, suggesting his run across Canada to raise money for research into cancer.

*Above:* **About 150 students visit the Terry Fox Centre each week. Here, they have an educational and fun experience, which they remember for long afterward.**

## His Name Lives On

Terry Fox was awarded Canada's highest decoration, the Order of Canada, and other awards both before and after his death. His biggest legacy to Canada is the many institutions and organizations started in his name. One of these, the Terry Fox Centre in Ottawa, was founded by an organization called the Council of Canadians, to provide a place for young people from all over Canada to come together and get to know one another better.

During the school year, students arrive in Ottawa from all parts of the country to work together on a Canadian theme, such as law and order, arts and culture, or science and technology. They attend talks and presentations, meet with experts in their field of interest, and spend time learning about one another and the parts of the country they come from. At the end of the week, they have established new friendships and have gained a better understanding of what Canada is all about — something Terry Fox himself would have been proud to be a part of.

# Totem Poles

## A Story to Tell

Totem poles, found in many parts of North America, are long vertical poles with intricate designs. Carved by the original native people, especially those on the west coast, the poles preserve their history and beliefs in visual form.

Many totem poles tell the story of an individual tribe, clan, or family. A clan totem can be a fish, animal, plant, natural object, or mythical beast, such as the thunder bird. This beast is believed to bring rain to prevent crops from drying. Some groups consider the totem to be the ancestor of their clan and have rules against killing or eating the animals carved on it.

*Opposite:* These totem poles show birds on the top. The carving of totem poles peaked in the early nineteenth century when good tools and money from the fur trade made it possible for the native chiefs to afford the poles.

## The Route to Totem Poles

The most intricately carved totem poles are found on Canada's west coast, where the Haida tribe lived. Many of the Haida totem poles were used as centerpieces for ceremonial occasions called potlatches. These important events were celebrated with huge feasts, special dances, and other ceremonies. Today, totem poles are in museums all over the country and in some special open air sites, such as the recreated Indian village of Ksann near Hazelton in British Columbia. The best overall collections are in the Canadian Museum of Civilization in Ottawa, on the campus of the University of British Columbia, and in Stanley Park, Vancouver.

*Left:* The Haida, seen here dancing in masks, were well known for their art. They carved elaborate totem poles with crests that represented important events in a family.

# Winter Carnival

## Snowman Reigns Supreme

A winter party, the *Carnaval du Québec* (car-na-val dew kay-BECK) has been held in Quebec City since 1954. Other cities in Canada have their own winter carnivals, but the Quebec Winter Carnival is the biggest of them all. People from all across Canada and from around the world gather here to be part of the extravaganza. The festival's symbol is a pudgy snowman in a red hat and woven belt. Called the *Bonhomme Carnaval* (bun-UM car-na-val), he springs to life during the carnival, appearing in most of the festival events, walking the streets, and taking pictures with eager adults and children.

## Winter Wonderland

The main attraction of Carnival is the crowning of the Festival Queen by *Bonhomme Carnaval* at a special ceremony. A new queen is chosen every year from among the many local girls that take part in the competition. A formal ball, held at Chateau Frontenac in Quebec, celebrates the crowning of the Queen. The *Soirée de la Bougie* (swah-ray de la boo-jee), meaning Night of the Candle, is another attraction of the festival. Thousands of candles add a glow to the city at night.

*Left:* **This castle is made out of ice! Many come to the Winter Carnival to admire it and to see other works of art in ice.**

## The Fun Is Just Beginning

Beside these events, there is a winter softball tournament, ice-wall climbing, a torch-lit ski parade, and a canoe race across the frozen St. Lawrence River from Quebec City to nearby Levis. One of the funniest events of Carnival is the snow bath. Despite freezing conditions, more than one hundred people parade in their bathing suits and roll around in the snow. They stop only when they can no longer stand the cold.

All of Quebec City is decked out in colorful decorations during the celebrations. The centerpiece is a huge Ice Castle made of more than twenty-five hundred blocks of ice. Surrounding it are hundreds of ice sculptures, made by Carnival participants. Teams from as many as twenty countries display their skills in the provincial, national, and international snow-sculpting demonstrations. Magical night parades with spectacular floats and amazing fireworks make this Carnival popular with the young and old.

*Above: Bonhomme Carnaval* **has a great time with visitors and participants, especially children. Here, to the delight of the children, he lends a hand in making a snowman.**

# RELATIONS WITH THE UNITED STATES

Canada and the United States were both settled along the Atlantic Coast in the early 1600s. Although it was the French who first took an interest in the country, by 1763 present-day Canada was a British colony like its neighbors to the south. However, unlike the United States, which gained independence from Britain in 1776, Canada remained under the British Crown much longer. On July 1, 1867, Canada became a nation and a democratic federation. Today, the United States and Canada are strong allies. Trade across the border is extensive, as is the sharing of ideas and culture.

*Opposite:* **Historic and modern buildings line the Halifax, Nova Scotia, waterfront. Thousands of Americans, mostly United Empire Loyalists, migrated north as a result of the American revolution (1775–1783), settling mainly on the empty shores of Nova Scotia.**

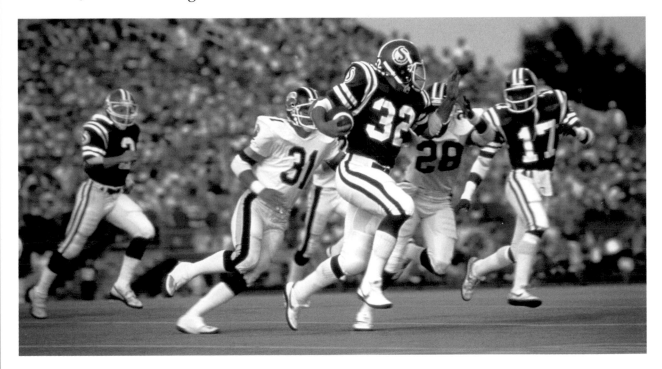

Both Canadians and Americans love sports. Canadians compete with Americans in baseball — an American game with a wide following in Canada, where it has been played professionally for over a century. However, only two Canadian professional teams — the Toronto Blue Jays and the Montreal Expos — compete with American teams in the World Series. The Toronto Blue Jays won the series in 1992 and 1993, in spite of the fact that some members of the team came from South America and the United States.

*Above:* **Canadians and Americans have another thing in common — their love for football. Canadian football was brought to Canada by immigrants and was introduced to the United States by players from McGill University in 1874.**

# From Foes to Allies

The friendly relations at present between Canada and the United States took time to establish. Some of the very first people to come to Canada — the United Empire Loyalists — moved north from the United States at the time of the American Revolution. Shortly after, Canada and the United States fought a war — the War of 1812 — in which ships from both sides shot at each other on the waters of the Great Lakes. The Americans pillaged the city of York. The war ended with the Treaty of Ghent in 1814. By this treaty, Britain and the United States agreed to demilitarize the Great Lakes and extend the border along the 49th parallel to the Rocky Mountains.

Relations became friendly again, but Canadians continued to worry about the growing influence of the United States — that it would tempt some of the struggling Canadian provinces away

*Left:* **A Loyalist settlement at York (now Toronto) in Upper Canada, 1804.**

*Above:* **The Arctic, with ice and glaciers, is difficult for ships to pass through.**

from their traditional loyalties to Britain and the Queen. This was one of the main reasons why the four eastern provinces of British North America were unified to create the Dominion of Canada. It also explains Prime Minister Macdonald's eagerness to build a railway, connecting the east and the west. He hoped to tempt British Columbia into joining the Confederation and prevent any empty land in between from falling into the hands of Americans.

## Friendly Seas

The Northwest Passage lies within the Arctic region of Canada and is blocked by ice almost all year. For many years, large ships found it difficult to make a crossing via this passage. Though some ships had attempted the north-west crossing before 1969, and three of them had succeeded, many had failed. In 1969, the United States sent the supertanker, USS *Manhattan*, through the Northwest Passage. It attempted to become the first commercial ship to make a successful crossing. Canadians were generally concerned that their sovereignty in the Arctic would be violated if a ship from the United States was the first commercial vessel to cross successfully, but in a display of goodwill, the Canadian government sent the icebreaker *John. A. Macdonald* to ensure a successful crossing.

# In War and Peace

When Canada or the United States or one of their allies is threatened by an enemy, Canadians and Americans readily lend a helping hand. This was true in both World War I and World War II. Canada joined the British in fighting the Germans in 1939 by sending soldiers to Europe. Two years later, thousands of American soldiers joined the Canadians and the British.

When Iran seized the American Embassy in Teheran in 1979, it held a few American diplomats as hostages, refusing to release them. Some Americans managed to escape to the Canadian embassy, where Canadian ambassador, Kenneth Taylor, gave them protection. Eventually, they were smuggled out of the country and returned to the United States. Similarly, when the United States led the Gulf War against Iraq's Saddam Hussein, Canadian navy warships patrolled the seas around the Persian Gulf to prevent guns and other weapons from being smuggled into Iraq.

In non-military matters, Canada and the United States have cooperated on trade-related issues. On January 1, 1989, a free-trade agreement between Canada and the United States took effect, and custom duties paid by Canadians on all purchases made in the United States were reduced under a timetable agreed on by the two governments. Canada and the United States also work together to put an end to drug smuggling. The Federal Bureau of Investigation in the United States and the Royal Canadian Mounted Police combine forces to prevent illegal drugs from being smuggled into the respective countries.

*Above:* **Kenneth Taylor became a hero when he successfully smuggled six U.S. diplomats out of Iran. He was awarded the U.S. Congressional Medal of Honor and the Order of Canada.**

*Opposite:* **Some consumer goods, such as skates and skis, had duties lifted immediately when NAFTA came into effect in January 1994. Under the NAFTA agreement, all customs duties between Canada, Mexico, and the United States will eventually be eliminated.**

*Left:* **Canadian recruits receive their first instruction in a military drill in 1939.**

## The Space Frontier

One area of active cooperation between Canadians and Americans is the conquest of space. Canadian scientists have worked on the American space program, while the Canadian Space Agency has sent several of its astronauts into space on U.S. space shuttles. The Canadarm — a crane-like device used in every shuttle mission to grab objects in space and release new ones — is an ingenious product of cooperation between the two countries.

## Leaders Set the Tone

Since 1867, Canadian prime ministers have made it a point to maintain friendly relations with the presidents of their neighbor to the south. In 1985, for example, Prime Minister Brian Mulroney invited U.S. President Ronald Reagan to visit him in Canada, where the two leaders — both of whom had Irish ancestors — sang the song, "When Irish Eyes are Smiling." During the Iran-Iraq War of 1980, President George Bush was in constant contact with Mulroney about the developments in the Gulf. Current Prime Minister Jean Chrétien has gone on fishing trips with President Bill Clinton. It was time well spent in improving the good ties that exist between the countries.

*Below:* Jean Chrétien, who was a lawyer before entering politics, became the prime minister of Canada in 1993. When overfishing became a problem on the northern Pacific coast of Canada and the United States, Chrétien and Bill Clinton agreed to settle it amicably with the help of an independent mediator. Presently, however, there is a lawsuit between British Columbia and the U.S. states of Washington and Oregon over salmon fishing rights on the west coast.

*Left:* **Celine Dion's album,** *Falling Into You*, **has so far sold twenty-four million copies worldwide. It won the Grammy for Album of the Year in 1997. Several biographies about Dion, who is thirty years old, detail the French Canadian's rise to stardom.**

## Songs Break Down Barriers

The hit song "Beauty and the Beast" from the Disney movie of the same title was the result of a joint creative effort between Canadian singer Celine Dion and American singer Peabo Bryson. In fact, many Canadian and American singers have worked together and produced popular songs. Dion has just recently released the duet, "Tell Him" with Barbra Streisand, while Streisand has sung, "I've Finally Found Someone" with Bryan Adams for the soundtrack of her movie, *The Mirror has Two Faces*. Canadians Anne Murray, Ronnie Hawkins, and Shirley Eikhard have, together with American musicians, received great acclaim for their performances.

# In Each Other's Countries

Canadians love traveling, and their most popular destination is the United States, accounting for more than 90 percent of all trips abroad. Its proximity, attractions, and the fact that some things are generally cheaper there than at home, make the neighbor to the south a natural getaway. Similarly, many Americans find going to Quebec to enjoy all things French is a cheaper alternative than traveling to France.

A drive in Canada, especially in the summer, usually means seeing hundreds of cars with American license plates on the roads. Some belong to Americans in Canada on business or work-related matters — Americans form the biggest number of expatriates in Canada, some 626,600 of them. But many vehicles are motor homes or campers driven by Americans who have come to Canada simply to see the country. Similarly, camp sites in Florida fill with Canadian motor homes in the winter. Many go to the southern United States to escape the bitter cold of Canadian winters. Some older, retired Canadians stay in Florida the entire winter — from November until March. Because they live half a year in the United States and half the year in Canada — "flying" to the south in winter — they are called "snowbirds."

*Below:* **One of the many American motor homes in Canada.**

## Students and Stars

Many Canadian and American students study in each other's country. McGill University, one of the most well-known universities in Canada, has large numbers of American students on its campus in Montreal, while Harvard, a prestigious American university, attracts many Canadian students to its campus in Cambridge — including the daughter of former Canadian Prime Minister Brian Mulroney.

There are also exchange programs and special events that attract students and adults in both countries. High school students, for instance, travel across the border for band or sports competitions. Many Canadians go south to be part of special events, such as the Mardi Gras in New Orleans. Americans also go north in large numbers to Canadian festivals, such as the Quebec Winter Carnival and the Calgary Stampede.

Canadians like watching popular American programs on Canadian television as well as going to the movie theaters to see American movies. The popularity of American movies results in some Canadians emigrating to the United States to advance their acting careers. The late John Candy, a famous comic actor, was born in Canada, as was Michael J. Fox who played Alex Keaton in the hit sitcom, *Family Ties.* He also played the role of a teenager sent back in time in the *Back to the Future* trilogy. Matthew Perry, who plays Chandler Bing in *Friends*, lived in Ottawa for many years before moving to the United States.

*Above:* **William Shatner (*left*) made a name for himself playing Captain Kirk in *Star Trek*, while Michael J. Fox (*right*) currently stars in the popular sitcom, *Spin City*.**

## Neighborly Differences

Canada and the United States are drawn close by free-trade pacts that see U.S. $1 billion a day in trade crossing the border. Although relations between the two countries are friendly, new restrictions on border crossings and trade conflicts over Pacific salmon fishing are problematic issues that are currently under negotiation. Canada has also disagreed with the United States over the embargoes placed on Cuba.

A potential new U.S. law will require Canadians to fill out forms or have a registered "smart card" when crossing the border after September 1998. The new law is meant to track noncitizens who cross the Mexican border, but Canadians, who for years crossed the border without filling out any forms, are not happy. Americans were also disturbed when an Alaskan passenger ferry was blocked from sailing for several days in 1997 by angry Canadian salmon fishermen to protest what they felt was overfishing by Alaskans. An American envoy to Canada best summed up the solution to these problems: "In virtually every instance, we have the same goal in mind. Sometimes, it just takes a little effort to get there."

*Below:* A female sockeye salmon waits patiently for a spawning mate. Canada and the United States have recently been battling over salmon such as these, which fetch a high price on the market. In 1997, Bill Clinton threatened in a letter to use the strength of the United States to retaliate against Canadians who protest that Alaskans are overfishing. Another area of disagreement between the countries is the failure of the United States to sign an international treaty banning land mines.

# Identity

The United States has had a strong influence on Canada in many ways. Former Prime Minister Pierre Trudeau, in a speech in 1969, best captured the influence that the United States has on Canada: "Living next to you is in some ways like sleeping with an elephant; no matter how friendly and even-tempered the beast, one is affected by every twitch and grunt."

Canada and the United States may seem to have similar cultures, and individuals may appear to be essentially the same. Canadians and Americans speak alike, dress alike, and have a similar lifestyle. Yet, the observant eye can see substantial differences between the two countries, especially in the way Canadians and Americans function in everyday life. For instance, Canadians are more community oriented in their personal lives and their work, and in other situations where membership in a specific group is considered important. One of the reasons for this is that while Americans pride themselves on and rejoice in being independent individuals, Canadians see themselves more as individuals within a group setting. Canadians also see themselves as a less mobile people, more rooted to their communities.

*Top:* **Americans visiting Canada are generally surprised to see Canadians walking the streets at night. This is possible because the crime rate in Canada is significantly low.**

*Above:* **Pierre Trudeau, former prime minister of Canada.**

**A**       **B**       **C**       **D**

**1**

ARCTIC OCEAN

Ellesmere
Island

BEAUFORT
SEA

ALASKA
(U.S.A.)

**2**

Yukon River

● Dawson
Klondike

YUKON
TERRITORY

Whitehorse ■

PACIFIC
OCEAN

Mount Logan
(19,524 ft/5,951 m)

NORTHWEST
TERRITORIES

Victoria
Island

Baffin
Island

NUNAVUT
(from 1999)

● Yellowknife

**3**

COASTAL MOUNTAINS

ROCKY MOUNTAINS

Cariboo
Mountains

BRITISH
COLUMBIA

ALBERTA

SASKATCH-
EWAN

Hudson
Bay

Jasper
National
Park

Vancouver
Island

Jasper ■

Banff
National
Park

Lake Louise

● Edmonton

MANITOBA

ONTARIO

**4**

Vancouver ●

Victoria ●

Columbia River

● Banff

Calgary ●

● Saskatoon

● Winnipeg

Lake Superior

● Sudbury

Ottawa River

**5**

UNITED STATES

Great
Lakes

Lake Huron

Niagara River
Niagara Falls

Lake
Michigan

● Toro

Stratford ●
London ●

Lake Erie

# CANADA

GREENLAND
(Denmark)

Arctic Circle

E F

ATLANTIC
OCEAN

NEWFOUNDLAND

QUEBEC

Labrador

Island of
Newfoundland

St. John's

St Lawrence River

Gulf of Saint
Lawrence

Gaspé
Peninsula

ST. PIERRE AND
MIQUELON
(France)

Charlottetown

Quebec

NEW
BRUNSWICK

PRINCE
EDWARD
ISLAND

Montreal

Saint
John

Ottawa

St Lawrence
Seaway

Appalachian
Mountains

Halifax

NOVA SCOTIA

N

Kingston

Lake Ontario
Horseshoe Falls

Annapolis
Royal

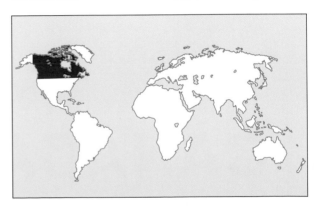

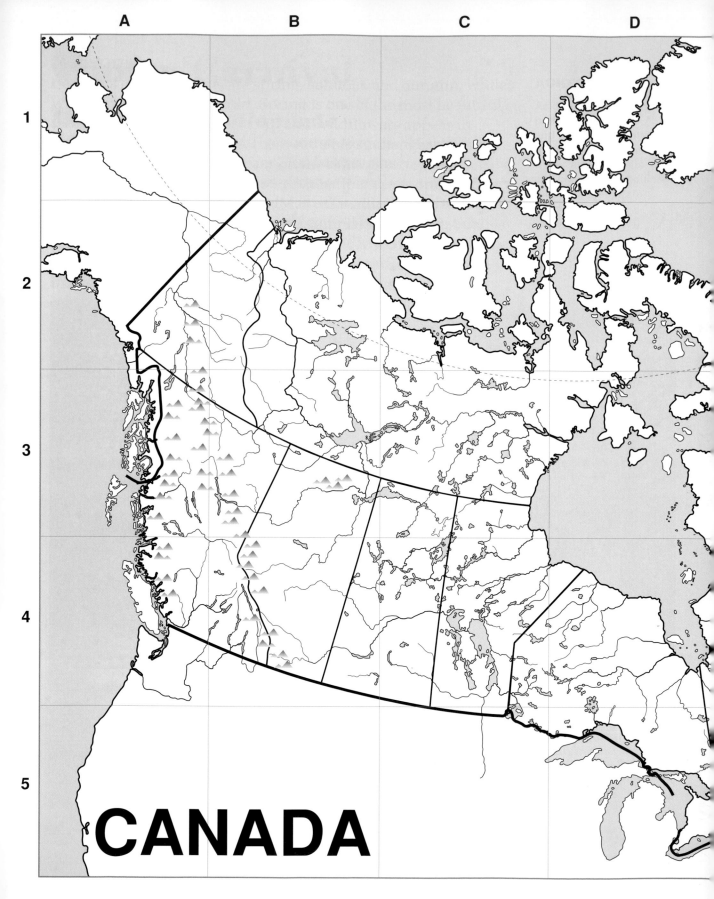

**CANADA**

# How Is Your Geography?

Learning to identify the main geographical areas and points of a country can be challenging. Although it may seem difficult at first to memorize the location and spelling of major cities or the names of mountain ranges, rivers, deserts, lakes, and other prominent physical features, the end result of this effort can be very rewarding. Places you previously did not know existed will suddenly come to life when referred to in world news, whether in newspapers, television reports, or other books and reference sources. This knowledge will make you feel a bit closer to the rest of the world, with its fascinating variety of cultures and physical geography.

Used in a classroom setting, the instructor can make duplicates of this map using a copy machine (PLEASE DO NOT WRITE IN THIS BOOK!). Students can then fill in any requested information on their individual map copies. Used one-on-one, the student can also make copies of the map on a copy machine and use them as a study tool. The student can practice identifying place names and geographical features on his or her own.

# Canada at a Glance

| | |
|---|---|
| **Land Area** | 3,800,000 square miles/9,900,000 square km |
| **Highest Point** | Mount Logan (19,524 feet/5,951 m) |
| **Largest Freshwater Lake** | Lake Superior (31,700 square miles/82,100 square km) |
| **Longest River** | Mackenzie, Northwest Territories |
| **Population** | 29,615,000 (1995 census) |
| **Population Distribution** | 76.6 percent in urban areas and 23.4 percent in rural areas |
| **Capital City** | Ottawa |
| **Provinces** | Newfoundland, Prince Edward Island, Nova Scotia, New Brunswick, Quebec, Ontario, Manitoba, Saskatchewan, Alberta, British Columbia |
| **Territories** | Yukon and Northwest Territories |
| **Major Religions** | Roman Catholicism, Anglicanism, Buddhism, Islam |
| **Official Languages** | English and French |
| **National Anthem** | "O Canada" |
| **National Motto** | *Ad mari usque ad mare* ("From sea to sea") |
| **National Flag** | Red and white stripes with a red maple leaf in the center. |
| **National Festivals** | Canada Day (July 1), Thanksgiving (second Monday in October) Christmas Day (December 25), New Year's Day (January 1), Easter (March/April), Victoria Day (fourth Monday in May). |
| **National Symbols** | Red Maple (Flora), Beaver (Fauna), Canada Goose (Bird) |
| **Current Governor General** | Roméo LeBlanc |
| **Current Prime Minister** | Jean Chrétien |
| **Currency** | Canadian dollar (C$ 1.43 = US $1 as of 1998) |

*Opposite:* **Lake Louise is found in Banff National Park, Alberta. It was originally called Emerald Lake. Queen Victoria renamed it after her daughter, Princess Louise, who married a Canadian governor general.**

# Glossary

## French & Native Vocabulary

*baggataway* (ba-gat-teh-WAY): a native game that developed group discipline and personal ingenuity. It was soon developed into lacrosse.

*Bonhomme Carnaval* (bun-UM car-na-val): a snowman in a red hat and sash that comes to life during the Quebec Winter Carnival.

*Carnaval du Québec* (car-na-val dew kay-BECK): a winter carnival in Quebec City that takes place in February.

*coureurs des bois* (koo-rer de bwah): illegal fur traders of the late seventeenth century.

*Kebec* (ke-BEK): an Algonquian Indian word for Quebec that means "place where the river flows."

*powwow* (PAU-wau): a meeting of Canada's native people that celebrates their history and culture.

*tortiere* (tor-tee-EHR): a kind of meat pie made of pork, which is a special food of Quebec.

## English Vocabulary

**acid rain:** precipitation with a high concentration of sulfuric and nitric acids that contaminates lakes and affects plants, animals, and humans.

**allophone:** a person whose first language is neither English nor French.

**anglophone:** a person whose first language is English.

**animism:** the belief that plants, animals, and any natural objects possess spirits.

**appliqué:** the art of sewing fabric shapes onto larger pieces of cloth.

**bluff:** a steep cliff or bank, usually situated by a river.

**Calgary Stampede:** a rodeo held in the second week of July. Cowboys compete in popular rodeo sports, such as wild horse racing and steer wrestling.

**Canadian Shield:** one of the world's largest geologic continental shields with extremely ancient rock.

**chuckwagon:** wooden cart that cowboys used when they were out on the open range.

**Confederation:** the union of New Brunswick, Nova Scotia, and the Province of Canada on July 1, 1867 that was called the Dominion of Canada. Manitoba, Saskatchewan, British Columbia, Newfoundland, and Prince Edward Island later joined in.

**correspondence course:** a course in which a student studies at home, receives assigments by post, and sends them back by post.

**daredevil:** a person who enjoys doing things or performing stunts that are very dangerous.

**evangelism:** teaching Christianity to people who are not Christians.

**expedition:** a journey that is usually long and has a specific purpose, such as exploration.

**fiddleheads:** young shoots of ostrich ferns that are steamed, boiled, or served cold in salads.

**francophone:** a person whose first language is French.

**gold rush:** a large and hurried movement of people to an area where gold has been discovered.

**Haida:** Indians of British Columbia who were known widely for their art, especially their beautifully carved totem poles.

**House of Commons:** the lower house of parliament in which elected members debate and present new laws.

**icebreaker:** a specially-built ship for frozen waters, which breaks the ice and creates a passage so that other ships can sail through.

**Inuit:** descendants of the original inhabitants of the Arctic regions of Canada and Greenland. They were formerly called Eskimos, which is now sometimes considered an offensive word.

**legislature:** the parliament of a province in which elected members debate and present new laws for that province.

**Maritime Provinces:** the provinces of New Brunswick, Nova Scotia, Prince Edward Island, and Newfoundland.

**Mennonite:** a strict Christian who lives according to the teachings of Menno Simmons, a Dutch Protestant leader.

**muskeg swamps:** areas of wet, spongy ground that usually have mosses, sedge, and stunted black spruce.

**NAFTA:** the acronym for the North American Free Trade Agreement. It was signed in 1994 and is meant to create greater economic ties between Canada, the United States, and Mexico.

**New France:** the name of the French-occupied region of North America until 1763.

**orca:** a killer whale.

**permafrost:** grounds in the Arctic region that remain permanently frozen.

**potlatch:** a ceremony of feasting and dancing in which a tribal chief gives gifts to his guests.

**prairie:** a large, flat, grassy area. The prairies in Canada are the southern parts of Alberta, Saskatchewan, and Manitoba.

**prime minister:** the leader of a country.

**seadoo:** watercraft for traveling on lakes and rivers.

**Senate:** the upper house of parliament in which senators appointed by the prime minister debate and approve new laws.

**separatism:** a movement or activities by people within a country who want their own government.

**skidoo:** a car-like machine with tracks like a tank that travels on snow. It is also called a snowmobile.

**spigot:** a special tap put into the trunks of maple trees that controls the flow of sap into a bucket.

**sugar bush:** a grove of sugar maples.

**sugaring off:** the collection of sap from sugar maple trees and its celebration as a festival in March and April.

**totem pole:** a carved and painted log that depicts the animals and spirits of the Indians in northwestern Canada. There are seven kinds of totem poles.

**United Empire Loyalists:** Americans who supported the British during the American Revolution.

# More Books to Read

*British Columbia.* Vivien Bowers (Lerner Publications)

*Canada.* David Marshall and Margot Richardson (Thomson Learning)

*Canada Celebrates Multiculturism. The Lands, Peoples and Cultures* series. Bobbie Kalman (Crabtree Publishing)

*Canada: The Culture. The Lands, Peoples and Cultures* series. Bobbie Kalman (Crabtree Publishing)

*The City Girl Who Went to Sea.* Hausherr, Rosmarie (Four Winds Press)

*Discovering Canada: The Fur Traders.* Robert Livesey and A. G. Smith (Stoddart Publishing)

*Canada. Festivals of the World* series. Bob Barlas and Norm Tompsett (Gareth Stevens)

*Klondike Fever: The Famous Gold Rush of 1898.* Michael Cooper (Clarion Books)

*Northwest Territories.* Richard Daitch (Lerner Publications)

*Quebec.* Hamilton, Janice. (Lerner Publications)

*The Story of Canada.* Janet Lunn (Lester Publishing and Key Porter Books)

# Videos

*Canada.* (International Video Network)

*Canada.* (Eastman Kodak Co.)

*Canada, True North: People and Culture.* (Encyclopædia Britannica Educational Corp.)

*Last Train Across Canada.* (Atlas Video)

# Web Sites

www.calgary-stampede.com/

www.cs.cmu.edu/Unofficial Canadiana/

www.onramp.ca/~lowens/107kids.htm

www-nais.ccm.emr.ca/schoolnet/

Due to the dynamic nature of the Internet, some web sites stay current longer than others. To find additional web sites, use reliable search engines with one or more of the following keywords to help you locate information on Canada. Keywords: *Canadian history, Quebec, acid rain, Niagara Falls, snowmobile, Terry Fox, Donovan Bailey.*

# Index